Praise for *How to Survive the Apocalyse*

What is a poem but a prayer? A sermon in verse, writ large and clear and Black for all to see? Black poets have always told the truth with God in one hand and blood in the other, and Jacqueline Trimble sits squarely in that tradition with *How to Survive the Apocalypse*. Her poems, which come from the gut, which come from the throat, which come from the beating heart of a Black woman making meaning out of the soured meal of America, are a wonder to behold. This book has no time for tea-party pleasantries or the curling of a politician's, or legal document's, or colonizer's tongue. It is a book of urgency and ultimatum—get on board, or get behind us.
> — Ashley M. Jones, Poet Laureate of Alabama,
> author of *Reparations Now!*

"*How to Survive the Apocalypse* has a lot of spark. It has a jazz quality. Or, more specifically, it speaks to what Art Blakey observed: 'Jazz washes away the dust of everyday life.'"
> — Nick Makoha, author of *Kingdom of Gravity*

In *How to Survive the Apocalypse* you will be lyrically captivated by Jacqueline Trimble, who reminds us what it means to "poet" in the twenty-first century. Not since Carolyn Rogers have we heard a voice this bold buttressed by poetic craft. It's all here—the energy and excitement of Black idiom reimagined as contemporary art, the beautiful defiance of a balled fist disguised as love. *How to Survive the Apocalypse* is so damn good it'll make you cry, not just because of some innate sadness in the words, but because these are bomb-poems, exquisite poems with teeth, cutting through the fat meat straight to the bone. Trimble aims straight at the heart of American life, and her beautiful poetic critique hits the bullseye.

— Randall Horton, recipient of the American Book Award for *#289–128: Poems*

Jacqueline Trimble's *How to Survive the Apocalypse* is a delicate kind of magic. This is a book that revels in a present and a future so rooted in history that it rhymes. Trimble's poems and stories remind us that apocalypse, for many of us, has been our primary inheritance. This is a collection that sings of all Black folks have endured in this country, not simply as a celebration of that endurance but as a righteous rejection of its continued necessity. I am so thankful for this collection.

— Nate Marshall, author of *Finna*

In *How to Survive the Apocalypse*, Jacqueline Trimble has crafted a powerful, clear-eyed guidebook for navigating the world. By turns witty and wry, these sharply observed poems ask us to consider the thin veil between past and present, between memory and truth. 'Do you see how we survived?' asks Trimble in 'The Fire Shut Up in My Bones.' These remarkable poems tell us and teach us. An extraordinary book.

— Catherine Pierce, Poet Laureate of Mississippi, author of *Danger Days*

"If you haven't lived through trials and tribulations, baby," the old folks would say, "just keepa living." Jackie Trimble's volume is about life and living. It is a personal, familial, communal, and ancestral testimonial swathed in joy and righteous indignation. These poems reveal the souls of Black folks ignited, renewed, and persisting in the face of injustice.

Trimble's words, images, and rhythms constitute a feast of uplift. And no matter whether they are served grilled, barbecued, baked or broiled, they are recipes for life, giving us new reasons to keep on living.

— Neal A. Lester, professor of English, founding director, Project Humanities, Arizona State University

"In the great American tradition of how-to manuals, we now have Jacqueline Allen Trimble's *How to Survive the Apocalypse*, a fast-moving meditation on what plagues us in our cities, our homes, and our relationships, especially the racial relationships that a black woman, with black children, in Montgomery, Alabama, has navigated. Trimble begins with family history and then detonates her way to the present moment. Read these poems and be convinced that the social apocalypse is upon us and is not going away. But there is a survival switch to be thrown—poetry at every turn that will not let go of shattering memories but will remake us if we allow the transformation. Trimble gazes straight into our eyes, challenges us to heed the warning truth, and skiddley-doos down the street, saying follow me! Read this book—for your own sake."

— Jeanie Thompson, author of *The Myth of Water: Poems from the Life of Helen Keller*

How to Survive the Apocalypse

ALSO BY JACQUELINE ALLEN TRIMBLE

American Happiness

How to Survive the Apocalypse

Poems

Jacqueline Allen Trimble

NewSouth Books

Montgomery

NewSouth Books
105 S. Court Street
Montgomery, AL 36104

Cataloging-in-Publication Data

Trimble, Jacqueline Allen
How to survive the apocalypse / Jacqueline Allen Trimble
p. cm
ISBN 978-1-58838-466-9 (trade cloth); ISBN 978-1-58838-476-8 (ebook)
1. Poetry. I. Title.

Library of Congress Control Number: 2022934636.

Design by Randall Williams. The cover art is by Carole Bandy Carson, © 2022.
Printed in the United States of America by Sheridan.

CREDITS

Many of the poems appeared in print previously. Thank you to all of the editors of these anthologies, journals and magazines who gave my voice a place to be heard. | "Even the Moon Must Have Troubles," in *The Night's Magician*, anthology, Negative Capability Press, Spring 2018. | "The First Will Be Last: A Parable," "Sonnet for Where We are Now," "My Daughter Says I Need Xanax: A Parable," and "Gunfight at the Neighborhood Grocery on Government Street," in *South Florida Poetry Journal*, November 2021. | "The Language of Joy," Poem of the Day in Poetry Daily, September 11, 2021; and as Duke University Hart Leadership Program's Poem of the Week, July 12, 2021, and originally in *Poetry Magazine*, July/August 2021. | "This is Why People Burning Down Fast Food Joints and Whatnot," "A Woman Cohabitates With Three Men," and "Poem for My Neighbor Whose Good Intentions are Wolf Pelt," in *Poetry Magazine*, July/August 2021. | "Kneeling is No Longer an Option" and "Running in America," in *Dove Tales: Writing for World Peace,* "Resistance" edition, September 2020. | "Oh, Say Can You See," in *Portside*, December 2018, and originally in *Poet Lore* 111, No. 3/4 Fall/Winter 2018, along with "Allies," "Counting Race," "How to Survive the Apocalypse," "My Son Says the Moon Landing Was a Lie," "Nat Turner Returns for His Stole Parts and Finds a Sermon of Rage," "Oh, Say Can You See," "Parable," "We Was Girls Together," and "World Economics," in the Poets Introducing Poets feature curated by Honorée Fanonne Jeffers. | "What If the Supreme Court Were Really the Supremes" and "Motherhood," in *The Louisville Review*, Fall 2017. | "Details," published in *The Rumpus* 2022 National Poetry Month project.

For my family —
Joseph, Joshua, Joseph David, II, Jasmine & Elijah;

for my mothers —
Billie, Cleola, Erna, and Marybelle;

and for the ancestors.

You are the key to my survival.

CONTENTS

PREFACE

When I was a child, my father owned a Masonic bible that sat alone on a small table in the living room of our house. A doily or some type of embroidered white cloth lay underneath it as if the book were enshrined. The nearby lamp cast it in a heavenly glow, and it seemed to throw off a power so great I was afraid to touch it or look at it too long. Is this true? Did the object itself burn this vision into my imagination or did my parents say, "Don't touch," as they often did to save precious things from grubby fingers. I only know for certain the bible was huge, encased in a royal blue cover, which was probably faux or the contemporary vegan leather. There was an inset picture of a mountain, probably Ararat, or maybe a young Jesus giving his elders the what-for on the cover framed with gold flourishes. Inside were slick, colorful pictures of biblical characters, story scenes, parting clouds, and awe-inspiring, ominous landscapes. Though this bible always scared me, I kept it, long after my parents were dead, unable to throw it away, certain, if I did, something from the sky would strike me dead where I stood. I carried it with me into adulthood, from one house to the other, my personal ark of the covenant, and it wasn't until my husband donated it to a local university archives that I was finally rid of this terrifying version of the word of God. Now, I wish I had it back. Not only because it also contained a history of my family's births and deaths, but also because I wish to hold it in my hands, examine it, discover the power it held over me for so long. It was probably Revelations, the troubling book at the end, that scared me most, that offered the most frightening pictures when I dared look. No one in Sunday School or church ever quoted this book that tells of the horrors to come at the end of the world—the plagues, the unrelenting horsemen, the judgment of God sending the righteous to heaven and the wicked into the tortuous pit. Though, why I would be afraid of that story is beyond me. Nothing in that bible has ever been as scary as what I have already survived, what my people have already survived again and again with only the imagined heaven of spirituals in sight.

Truth is, the world is always ending in one way or the other. I was born on a dark and stormy night, a clichéd opening that was really the ending to something else, the story of a stern but repentant grandmother, having tossed my pregnant mother out, and an uncle who, delayed by a bridge washed away in the weather, did not make it to the hospital before my new adoptive parents came to claim me. Papers signed. The end. New story. Four years later that adoptive mother died of breast cancer, another ending. A few years after that my father married again and we moved from the farm to the city and then he died too, leaving me with the third mother of my life all before I was seven. And yet, there I was in my own story, a child reading poetry, reading everything I could find, making things—clothes, doilies, paintings, music, dances—as fast as I could, using the force of my imagination to keep it all going. The end of the world kept coming—sudden, dramatic change. Loss. The violation of the body, death of a boyfriend, death of another mother, of a friend. I had to create my way into survival and out of erasure. I had to outrun the horsemen in that damn blue bible or be judged into annihilation. And yet nothing is ever lost in the universe; it is merely transformed into something else like spirituals, sorrow songs, the blues or poetry. How many slave narratives are just survival tales on their way to better times? How many endings have been gathered into the squares of quilts, making something new and useful from remnants of the old life? We create to keep living, to know we are still alive.

When I was growing up Jim and Viola Williams babysat me every day after school until my mother came home from work. We had coffee made on a gas heater in their front bedroom that was also their living room. Mine was more evaporated milk and sugar than coffee, but I loved our ritual. Mr. Williams sat in his chair and smoked a pipe. Mrs. Williams and I talked about how crazy the people were on the soap operas, which she called her "stories," and each of us offered what we figured would happen next. Sometimes Mrs. Williams and I sat on the porch and played Old Gray Horse. We pulled the leaves off the bushes within our reach, and hid them in our fists. One would say, "Old gray horse!" And the other would say, "I ride him." The first would say, "How many miles?" Then the rider would have to guess how many leaves the first speaker held. The leaves were the miles. And a correct guess, would earn the other's leaves as reward. The one with the most at the end won. Mrs. Williams would always guess right, so sometimes I would let a few leaves drop out of my hand off the porch. She often caught me, but that was part of the fun of the game. Later, we would watch television until dinner time when my mother came to get me.

I didn't eat with them very often, but on the occasions I did, Mrs. Williams would fix my favorite dish of hers, turkey butts with gravy and spaghetti. Other times she made pig ears with mustard and white bread or neck bones and rice. It was always delicious. She taught me about the joys of onion salt and chicken thighs on the days she was being fancy, which always came near the first of the month. It never occurred to me these delicacies that I never got at home grew out of a need to make do with whatever was cheapest at the market. What did I know about adult economics?

They rented the house they lived in from my mother, and rarely had money for extras like a car or even a Christmas tree. By the time I came to understand, they had passed away. Mr. Williams died first. Mrs. Williams went to a nursing home when I was a teenager, and despite all she had done for me and despite my mother's urging, I only visited her once. And yet they are my ancestors. They are my kin. I can still taste the weird chocolate and imitation coconut candy they kept in a little tin on the bureau next to Mr. Williams's pipe tobacco. I am certain now they bought this as a treat for me. I didn't care for it though I dutifully took a piece when offered. I also cannot say I always liked going there. They were retired and very old. Mrs. Williams had been a practical nurse. Mr. Williams had been some sort of laborer, maybe a custodian. I could be a moody child, and I am sure I was a handful, especially when I was restless and I found the tedium of their routine boring compared to the rough and tumble fun of children riding bikes or skating up and down the sidewalk.

Looking back I see how extraordinary they were. Why didn't I have the sense to ask them more questions about themselves, what they had endured, how they had survived with their joy and humor intact? Where did the patience for this foolish child come from, even though they had never been able to have children of their own? They were the history of my people, and they were right there for me to absorb. I barely even listened to the stories they told me about themselves. Sometimes Mr. Williams would go on fiery political rants about celebrities of the time who had not supported civil rights, who had built careers on the backs of black talent and black patronage but had no interest in helping black people. He particularly hated Elvis Presley and would never let me watch his movies on principle. Still, they left so much of themselves with me—their love, creativity, activism. Their pride in being who they were. Were they an ending or a beginning?

Before 2012, the year the world was supposed to end for sure, I took some students on a trip to the Yucatan peninsula. There we met a Mayan guide who told us we had the wrong idea. The end of the world was not just destruction, but a starting over, a renewal, a rebirth. "The world will cast off the old and be made new," he said. "It will begin again." This story appealed to me. Even the apocalypse seemed a manageable thing, a thing where what we had survived would be destroyed, and we would begin again, creating a new world out of the remnant of the old one.

How to Survive
the Apocalypse

ONE

Lord have mercy on this land of mine
We all gonna get it in due time

— NINA SIMONE

PLAGUE

When it comes
as it always does
do as you are told,
abandon the schools and shops,
the arenas and churches.
Make a list. What can you live without?
Carry only what you can carry
into your bunker of a house,
the stockpiles of toilet tissue and disinfectant
lined up like children waiting to return
from recess. If you have forgotten
something, check your yard
or kitchen cabinets. Remember—garlic
treats the flu. Cinnamon can heal
the gut. Dandelion is a medicinal
miracle. Don't worry
if the only face you have seen
is your neighbor's peeking at you
from her window or if the quiet
is so quiet it sounds like prelude.
If you are brave
walk out into the thirsty streets.
Do not note the heaviness of the sky.
Do not listen for locusts or hoof beats.
This is just another evening
constitutional. Work, if there is work.
If not, meditate. Pretend your hunger

Plague

is fasting. Listen, Israelite,
you are lost in a manicured
wilderness. You should rethink
the necessity of touch. You should rethink
necessity itself.

WHAT IF THE SUPREME COURT
WERE REALLY THE SUPREMES?

Oh, how their bedazzled robes shine
as they glide into the courtroom,
open wide their satin-gloved arms, flutter
their long, store-bought eyelashes and croon,
"My world is empty without you, babe."

Even Cindy Birdsong envies their hips.
Pop and sway, dip and snap.
Each one a lady.
Would these judges made new
by the rhythm and the blues,
the ooh, ooh baby magic of a Motown spell,

ever hold the sequined fish of my voting rights
above their lovely bouffant heads,
tip its iridescent scales toward the camera,
then gut it like a dinner trout?

OH, SAY CAN YOU SEE

No refuge could save the hireling and slave
From the terror of flight or the gloom of the grave
— FRANCIS SCOTT KEY

Those slaves at Fort McHenry
never had a chance
to kneel.
Probably dead before
they hit the ground
like that boy shot
twenty times
his cell phone still
smoking in his hand
his grandmother's backyard
a burial ground
not sacred enough
nor was his body
a temple the cops
dare not enter.
Maybe if he had
wrapped himself in stars
and stripes, someone
would have unholstered
a hand, placed it
on the heart
and begun to sing.

Patriotic songs
of the brave:
Lift every voice
My soul looks back
Before I'll be a slave
I'll be buried
In my grave.
How many black bodies
must fall to hallow
these urban battlefields?
This is not a rhetorical
question. I am asking
for the exact body count.

SONNET FOR WHERE WE ARE NOW

My neighbor is stockpiling Tiki torches and shovels.
He waves like a salesman. Suspicious and friendly.
I wave back but do not smile. My son is sick and uninsured.
His cough is as deep as a sinkhole. My mother once entertained
a bomb shelter salesman. She bought a Cadillac instead.
Drove it to California. Drank lemonade under a lemon tree. I spend
sixty dollars at Whole Foods. Quinoa was food for the poor elsewhere.
My neighbor is keen on the wall. Hoards should be allowed nowhere.
Jesus has not been to our church since January. Strange.
My husband complains about no milk in the house. I am deranged
by the cost of everything. A sinkhole opens in my backyard.
My neighbor has never smiled so hard before.
Today he unloads more shovels. And rope.
Maybe we will get that pool we hoped for.

THE LAWS OF INSURRECTIONISTS

Remember, always, the 2nd amendment is prettier than the 1st.

Shoot (or beat if there are too many witnesses) any protestors
engaged in public displays of freedom if what is being protested
is contrary to your own thinking   ,
or the Internet.

Wear feathers and skins as a sign that anything
you can kill can be also be revered in retrospect
once it has been neutralized, assimilated, or
removed to parts unknown.

Call the cops on birdwatchers, brown folks grilling
hotdogs in public parks, and unwanted neighbors
just because this is still a free country
and you can.

Buy white vans and fertilizer, then blow everybody up.

If someone shoots elementary school children out of jealousy
or dresses as a superhero and assaults sitting patrons
in the movies, comfort yourself. What did I tell you
to always remember?

Hate abortion no matter what. Period.

Say blue lives, all lives, my life, our lives, he's got
the whole world in his hands, I don't see color or
whatever, but never ever say black lives matter lest
you be thought a socialistic, unpatriotic, tree-hugging
America-hating fool.

Don't be too intellectual. It's very unpatriotic and
particularly unattractive in women.

Champion, at all costs, public lynchings and executions,
restrictive voting laws, the military, and prisons.
In fact, sacrifice everything—education, health care,
your own kind—to build more prisons
as fast as humanly possible. You must take responsibility
for your family's safety.

Discredit science in favor of quackery and gut feelings.
Lean into your own understanding of whatever
you do not understand.

Do not let your children learn critical race theory.
Pilgrims settled America. George Washington's teeth
were wooden. Manifest Destiny was about God's will
for America from sea to shining sea. Those people
from Africa were immigrants.
Period.

Clean your guns on Wednesdays while listening
to talk radio and be sure to quote Martin Luther
King, Jr. to encourage non-violence among those
you might shoot.

When the popularity of your narratives fades
or there are too many commercials with interracial couples
or you suspect that the playing field is scheduled
to get leveled next Friday, riot, riot, riot.

Build gallows for your own who fail to follow
these laws at all times and in all ways
and think of yourself as a patriotic tourist
while you do.

Forget that patriotism is a form of love,
the deep, abiding kind that bears its breast
in a crowded bus station, makes four plaits
on one head, lies counting the vagaries of a lover's breathing
as a rosary, wears a mask, takes a bullet for kin and country,
or loves one's neighbor as oneself.

It is not that. Never, never that.

A POLICY STATEMENT OF WHAT WASN'T SAID

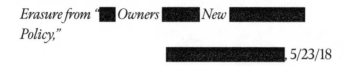

Erasure from " ▮ *Owners* ▮ *New* ▮
Policy,"

▮*, 5/23/18*

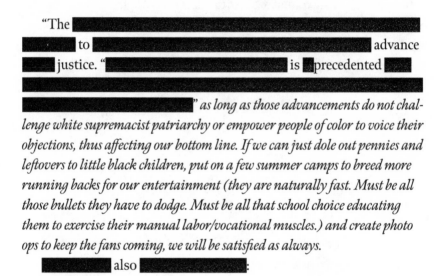

"The ▮
▮ to ▮ advance
▮ justice. " ▮ is ▮ precedented ▮
▮
▮ " *as long as those advancements do not chal-
lenge white supremacist patriarchy or empower people of color to voice their
objections, thus affecting our bottom line. If we can just dole out pennies and
leftovers to little black children, put on a few summer camps to breed more
running backs for our entertainment (they are naturally fast. Must be all
those bullets they have to dodge. Must be all that school choice educating
them to exercise their manual labor/vocational muscles.) and create photo
ops to keep the fans coming, we will be satisfied as always.*
▮ *also* ▮ :

1. ▮ personnel on the field ▮
   flag ▮ *whether you want to or not or whether the flag respects
   you. We own you, boys. We have the papers on you, bought and paid for
   your body, your soul and your rights.*

2. ▮ require ▮
   ▮ field ▮ Anthem *so as to keep up the pretense this is not about
   American greed, as always. If you want to protest, do it out of sight of all*

the fans who might be offended, of all the fans who might have to think about social justice, of all the fans who might have to look into these deaths. Somebody might have the power to change the system we love. After all, it is working as it is designed to work, as our forefathers intended.

3. ██████████████████████████ stay ████████████
██████ off ██ field until ██████████████████ *your freedom of speech has been violated.*

4. ██
show respect ███████████████ *the lies of our narrative. How can we keep this story going of home of the free if you ungrateful, rich, spoiled boys keep testifying otherwise?*

5. ████████████████ rules, ████████████████████
██ *because we believe in States Rights and a master's wisdom to discipline the slaves on his field as he sees fit.*

6. ████████████████ impose ████████ discipline on ████ personnel ██
████████████████████████████ *because we have to keep the overseers in line too lest they forget the mission.*

KNEELING IS NO LONGER AN OPTION

If I could fill up this whole sheet of paper
with rage, I would fill it up like this
rage, rage, rage, rage, rage,
or I could put rage to the 100th power
like mathematicians who want to express
a number that is too big so their hands will not
get tired of writing all the zeros plus
it is inefficient to write all those zeroes
like my rage is often inefficient when
I watch the news or look at social media
and I see people lying on my people and I see
my people trying to say what is true over and over
and over and over and over and over
and over to the 100th power and I see them
telling us there wouldn't be any problems
if we would respect, respect, respect
to the 100th power the flag and all the other institutions
that have been created to kill us to the 100th
power and I am Fannie Lou Hamer sick and tired
of being sick and tired and this rage is a laser
incinerating to the 100th power my insides
one cell at a time and that may not be scientific
but it is a statistical fact I will die younger
and suffer more chronic disease like

hypertension because to put all that pressure
on a body not made to withstand it
is like riding around on tires made for 32 psi
that are filled with 32 psi to the 100th power though
it is not physically possible to put that much
rage in a tire without it blowing up in your face.

ALLIES

I can't believe what you say, because I see what you do.
— JAMES BALDWIN

Thank you for letting me know
you voted for the black guy
you are sad when you think of segregation
you are angered by your family's attitude
you have boycotted businesses on my behalf
you never use that word
you disapprove of those who do
you protest Confederate monuments
you give to the NAACP
you have made many woke signs
you own tons of woke T-shirts
you never would have owned slaves
your parents taught you to love everybody
your father used to hire black workers
your mother marched with King
you loved your black maid
your black maid loved you
your favorite singer/actor/writer is black
you never see color
you have two black friends
your boyfriend/husband/girlfriend/wife/babymamadaddy is black
your child's best friend is biracial
you admire Oprah so much

you admire Beyoncé so much
you admire hip hop so much
you love that MLK
you wish you had my skin
you wish you had my hair
you wish you were a strong black woman
you have to have that sweet brown sugar
you had to tell your daddy he raped you
you have to keep peace with your neighbors
you have to keep peace at the office
you have to keep peace in your church
you have to stay true to your upbringing
you wish we would let it go
your grandfather did not know any better
when he grinned for the camera
beneath the charred body.

NAT TURNER RETURNS FOR HIS STOLEN PARTS
AND FINDS A SERMON OF RAGE

Nat Turner makes the slow trek through
the attics of America. He wishes
to pull himself together. He knocks on doors.
And the ones who answer clutch his parts like charms.
And the ones who answer call him "apparition,"
"ghost," "spook." No matter. Nights,
he creeps between the sutures of history
and takes himself back. Nat Turner walks
through America. He meets a black man.
"Hey, man, "How does your rage fare?"
The man says, "My rage is as coy
as public impotence
as long and blunt as a Billy stick
as black as a cruiser
as careless as a traffic stop
as pale and slender as hand-rolled cigarettes
as real as toy guns
as bloody as blood
on a white T-shirt
in the front seat of a paid-off hearse."
Nat Turner walks tall through America.
He meets a black woman. "Sister," he says,"
"How does your rage fare?"
"My rage," she says, "is a dragging by the hair,
a fissure in the head, a shuttered eye, a city-wide lie, Lord,
a you-shalt-not, a page-five story, a that's-my-baby,

a bomb unmoored.
My rage is dead girl smiling
a dead boy sagging, a dead man breathing,
a dead woman swinging.
It's as nimble, Lord, as a sassy tongue."
Nat Turner lifts his eyes to the hills.
The whole of him is avenging angel.
He absolves the wicked and blind with his sword.
"Lord," he prays, "Lord, Lord, Lord,
build a hedge of protection so high
we can't see a thing but our rage.
Let rage keeps us woke all night
and all day. Let us sharpen our daggers
on its whetstone. Let us lower our blades
again and again for mercy and love.
Our rage—yes, Lord—our rage
more powerful than despair,
able to leap tall headstones
for generations.
Hallelujah.
Amen."

THE FOUR HORSEMEN CAME TO TOWN
LAST TUESDAY

Before the locusts appeared
in India and the dust cloud drifted over
from Africa, the Four Horsemen arrived,
lost and off schedule, at the Stab and Go
Convenience Store on the corner. That's what we called it
because of the man who got stabbed there years ago. Nobody
remembers the details. Isn't that how myths are made?
The clerk would never forget this day.
How polite they were. Posing with the customers.
Buying maps. Getting their bearings. When asked
what was to come, they just smiled and shrugged.
Their horses pranced for two homeless veterans
who argued about their exact names, one preferring
the Old Testament, and the other insisting on the popular.
They agreed only on Death who waited patiently
at the corner. Always content in any direction.

GUNFIGHT AT THE NEIGHBORHOOD MARKET ON GOVERNMENT STREET

Public Safety Director James Barber told NBC 15 the shooting stemmed from an altercation between two men inside the Walmart Neighborhood Market on Government Blvd.
— From "MPD Release Identities of Two Killed in Mobile Walmart Shooting," Lindsey Bullard, NBC 15 News, Feb. 12, 2020

This was a story of small reckonings,
a ballad for the local news. Everybody wants to know
why, as if why could tell the tale any better
than those two dead men. Might as well say,

it was a cattle farmer who did not want sheep
grazing on his land, a no name claim jumper
called out. Somebody stole the love of somebody's life
without one sorry or pardon me. Does it matter?

What we know is the one who drew first
was in a wheelchair. One of them repented
before he died. The rest is just the B-line
from a *Bonanza* episode. Every week

those Cartwrights held class on good and evil.
No matter how bad the bad guy was, how fast a draw,
if Pa Ben fell down a mountain or Little Joe was pinned
by outlaws, when everything was hopeless

and impossible and lost, goodness brought them safely back
to the Ponderosa, and Hoss, that toothy giant,
tipped his big white hat, as if to say, class is dismissed
until next week. Simple. The bad guys, playing dead,

got up. Kinfolk dried their eyes. Everything was smiles
and let me buy you a drink. Who wouldn't want to be those boys?
We should have asked more questions—Why were all the mothers
of Ben's sons dead? How did Chinese people feel

about Hop Sing? Why are people armed
and dangerous in the grocery story? Truth is
shooters still exist in the world. And Ben and the boys
and those men at Walmart are dead. I hope

they are riding together in heaven. All over
a wild territory. Busting through a burning map,
those wagon spokes replaced by a wheelchair rim.
I hope the boys can see their mamas now,

that the Walmart men are telling them
they were too old to be living with their Pa.
Maybe pointing out how Hop Sing
should have been treated better. Got himself

a spouse. His own piece of land. A gun
and a horse too. Maybe they are telling them
what only the dead can tell. Nothing, not even killing
and dying, will ever be as simple as it's told.

PARABLE OF THE WOMAN AND THE PEACH TREES

FOR JM

This is a parable, which is to say
there is a lesson here that is not opaque,
since these are simple once upon a times
with simple meanings. And true. Like
true crime stories are true and like it is true

once, my peach trees budded in February.
How could they know they would die next week
when the deep frost came? What a beautiful,
sad tale. Duped by temporary spring,
a promise of warmth before the cold truth.

We used to say to lie was to tell a story. Yesterday,
a woman told me a true story about her life—
When she was a girl she fell in love with a girl,
and she was happy until her mother discovered
this unfolding and beat her until she learned
to lie, to tell the story a mother could bear

to hear, to say, *I was just playin',* which means
I was just lying, but not really. So she gave her kisses
to a man since the universe is propped up on lies
which inspire the dreams of young girls,
but this man she tried to love, to squint her eyes

and see as prince and squint harder to see herself
as princess, and squint even harder to see a possibly
forever happily, beat her as well, and after that
the next man, who seemed as if he loved her, beat her
when she told him she loved a woman. Like her mother,

he too preferred lies, and so at last she turned to a woman
who certainly loved her, but when this woman also beat her,
so hard only the sound of a daughter's voice pleading
for her life kept her alive, she called the law, which
everyone said was blind. *Surely there will be justice now*,

but the cop who came to see about her told her
to choose another narrative. *God intended you
for men. This is a sign. You should return
to a conventional story.* Beloved, what is this woman
to do? Die like a peach blossom, beautiful, embracing
a lie, or should she write her own story and live?

WORLD ECONOMICS

A man stands in the Kenyan desert. He
is not Kenyan, but a refugee. Both
guest and stranger, he claims no country, and
no country claims him. Not even the one
which stole him from his mother's care to make
him a soldier. He gazes toward the place
he once killed a man, and the place his wife
and children live without him. Behind him,
the world is made of thorns. His belly is
full of hunger. He has traded a day
of food for phone minutes. Each time he talks to
his wife is a morsel of bread. His child's
first steps were a bowl of rice. He wears a
lavender T-shirt. Disney World, it says.
Mickey Mouse smiles across the faded back-
ground. The woman who bought it lives in Ala-
bama. The daughter she picked it for lives
in Tennessee. The man in the Kenyan
desert has never heard of these states, but
he knows the place on his T-shirt is the
happiest place on earth. He posts a picture
of himself. He smiles and gives a thumb's up.
"Chillin' at Disney," he writes. Africa pretends
to be Epcot in the background. Here is a life
he can make for himself. The woman
who bought the shirt has never been
to Africa. She went to Haiti once.

A mission trip. There she saw a girl
making pies of government dirt,
sugar, water, something else. Thousands of pies.
She saw the people buy and eat the dirt. The girl
took the money the woman gave her. The woman
threw the pies in the hotel trash.
A woman drives down a boulevard in Alabama.
She is headed for Goodwill.
Her SUV is crammed with bags. Crammed
with discarded T-shirts. The joy of giving
wells up in her heart like the pride
a man who is not Kenyan feels. So many likes
and loves for his made-up vacation in America.

THIS IS WHY PEOPLE BURNING DOWN
FAST FOOD JOINTS AND WHATNOT

Q. How do others sin against you?
A. By cursing me—telling lies about me—or striking me.
Q. What must you do to those who thus sin against you?
A. I must forgive them. *

See, I learned my catechism well.
Learned to offer my cloak and coat, my cheek
again and again as the skin was splayed
from my body. I can quote
Martin Luther King, Jr. with ease,
praise the Americana of his martyrdom,
the sweet, unselfish beauty of that bullet's velocity.
Shall I sing *We Shall Overcome* while
I swing? I have wanted so long
to believe in justice, to think of each blow
as recompense for my wickedness.
How can I continue?
How can I continue?
How can I continue
to take and eat this image
of myself, choke on the eloquence
of my dissent, speak love fluently
to someone with his knee
on my neck, his bullet in my child?

*Catechism, To Be Taught Orally To Those Who Cannot Read; Designed Especially for the Instruction of the Slaves: Electronic Edition. Protestant Episcopal Church in the Confederate States.

DENOTATION FOR THE PEOPLE

When Spell Check redlined "lynchings"
as if that word did not exist

had not been defined forever
by fire and skin,

I hit "add to dictionary" so fast
I'm sure you felt the world
evolving.

SOME OF US WERE REAL REGULAR
AND THAT'S ALL RIGHT

I'd like to say my ancestors were noble people.
Part of the 1619 group. The first ground-
breaking-Benjamin-Banneker-Phillis-Wheatley-Peters
something. They were not. More of a peanut stew.
Smart. Alcoholic. Sometimes crafty
or criminal. Land tillers, steel workers,
Pullman porters, teachers. Bring the liquor
and the ribs on Saturday. Sit on the deacon's pew
or mind the doors with gloved hands
on Sundays. Weekdays saving dimes from two jobs
to send children to another life. These folks
would serve you tea on well-polished silver,
then take their shoes off
and make you call the police. No worse than most.
But, noble? I'm not going to lie
like some of you. I come from peasant stock.
Good. And otherwise.

BIOGRAPHIA BLACK WOMAN
LATE 19TH EARLY 20TH CENTURY

Lillian Brewster Dungee
1868–1939

Shall I begin with she was a Victorian woman? Although, what does that even mean given her context. Black. Southern. Daughter of formerly enslaved people in the Cradle of the Confederacy. What must she have thought of a Queen who colonized the world? Who used brown bodies to keep the Empire's sun shining? This girl child was born while the smell of the auction block lingered in her hometown. Cotton broker buildings still doing business. Did she ever pass by the people who owned her parents? Were they relatives? Is this a proper *biographia*? Shall I begin again? This is the history of a great woman, an ancestor's history, though she was not precisely my kin. Still, I call her ancestor, Lillian Brewster Dungee, a black woman, who lived and breathed and loved and died in Alabama where she was born to mother and father, formerly enslaved as house servants. She was educated at Talledega College and taught school until she married. What was that like, that long drive to the college? Did her father load up her belongings on a wagon? Did her mother go through the dark woods with them? A perilous journey? Many a dark man and dark woman has been lynched in those woods. Could they hear them screaming in the silence? Or was it a thoughtless journey? Ordinary as heat in summer. Maybe she took the train and the wagon and woods were small parts of the journey. How lovely it would be to sit in her parlor and ask her these questions. History says so little about what I need to know. I never knew her, but I know her because I grew up in the house, the proper Victorian house with its narrow hallway and pocket doors, she and her husband, Dr. Alfred Coleman Dungee, Sr., purchased. He was a doctor, one of the earliest black doctors in the state of Alabama, and she was his educated wife, a club woman, a leader of women. My mother was once her daughter-in-law before she married my father and became my mother. So it is Alfred Coleman Dungee, Jr., the child of Lillian Brewster Dungee, dead husband to my mother, who connects me to her, who provides the rope of kinship. A growing up among her things connects me as well. Her picture sits in my house. Her furniture, my inheritance, and though she was long, long dead before I was born, I know her by what remains: a comb she wore in her hair; the wax dance card on which she wrote; the loving cups and trays given to her for her club woman excellence. These are the artifacts of her life.

And then there are the stories. There was a rumor that she was a First Nations princess, and her skin was as pale as an underdone hoe cake. (Remember, her parents were recently enslaved. I do not know if that had something to do with her very pale skin, but her mother was equally as pale. I could draw a conclusion.) There was also this story of a young Northern white man who wanted to take her away with him and whose hand she refused. She married the black doctor instead. Lillian, though she would never have allowed me to call her that and I never would have dared, is the stuff of my dreams. Her pictures sit in my house, a daguerreotype of her and her mother, of her and the good doctor and their son. She is quite the lady in these pictures. Casual and rich. These pictures live in my dreams, my dreams, excavating the bits and pieces of her life, and her parents' dreams, shaping her into something they had not had a chance to be. What were her troubles, this upper-middle class black woman in a place where survival for black folks was as narrow as a sidewalk or as faint as a knock on the wrong door? What kept her up at night in the beautiful old bed that now belongs to my daughter? Was it that they were lynching people here and happy to do it? She was not happy they were doing it. Maybe it bothered her even more after her twins were born. (I know that feeling of unrelenting fear. Raising black children in a world that itches to turn blackness to ash.) A boy and a girl. The girl was solid, blonde and robust. That's what I have been told. The boy was weak and small. She didn't worry about the girl. It was the boy. And yet the girl died, and the boy became a doctor. He was a bookish boy. I know this because he left his books for me, though he did not know me. And I read them all. Spent my childhood gathering his aesthetic. Was it her aesthetic too? Surely his love for books came from somewhere.

When his father Dr. A.C. Coleman Sr. died in 1917, the boy was in medical school. Lillian must have been troubled about money because that's the year she got a job with the court. That's the year she became the first black person appointed to the Court of Domestic Relations, a position she held for more than twenty-five years. What? A black woman. In Alabama. In 1917. A job with the court. A job she created for herself. And they listened to her. Historians, there are court documents to prove it. A reform school she founded. Historians, there is a plaque to prove it. The legends she inspired. There are still old folks who remember her wheeling her big black car through the neighborhood. "Here come Miss Dungee," they cried. "Run!" Making sure the children go to school. Speaking up for them in court. Speaking out against lynching with the third Mrs. Booker T. Washington and the Negro Women's Federated Clubs. Historians, there are newspaper articles to prove it. And there is a club, still in existence, named after her. A force. A force. A force.

How did it all happen, Lillian? So many questions you have left my imagination to answer. Where has your story been all this time? Where have so many stories been all this time?

THE YOUNG WHITE GENTLEMAN
WANTS LILLIAN TO PASS AND BE HIS BRIDE

My white
    hand touches his white
hand. The space between us is a whiteness
                        so bright even his white
money and white
    name cannot absolve the white-made
distance. Love cannot white-out
          custom or law any more than the white-hot
intensity of his words, his white
    brow feverish with plans to run North. *Be reasonable,*
he says, as if reason resides in the white meat,
    as if our little white
lie could white-wash
    the drops of my black
    blood or I would ever sacrifice my deep black
heart and soul to him or exchange it for this mantle of white.

MY MAMA TRIES TO KEEP ME FROM THE BLUES

She did not dress me in linen,
grease down all undignified edges,
shod my clumsy feet in education,
fitted and laced, to have me moan
and tremble like a woman caught
with someone else's man.

You better cling to white Jesus, girl.

That music, coarse and kinked, smelling
of gin and smoke, a place to be from
and forget.

Put those gloved hands together
and pray.

But mama, a hymn is not enough.

Lord, deliver her from the blues
blaspheming way.

And even a spiritual, ripe with hallelujah,
cannot carry your cotton sack along
when the rent is due, the baby
is sick, and your man swings
to no music at all.

LILLIAN'S PRAYER FOR HER BOY CHILD

The girl was the strong one. Barging into
The world, a force already, not like her brother
we feared would not live. I held him
while his twin slept, my arms his swaddling
and his cradle. What prayer can I offer
for this boy child?

Dear God, keep him from this world
with its hunger for blackness. Mind his neck,
the crown of his head, the soles of his feet.
Teach him to run. Make him so fast no fire
Can scorch nor knife dismember. Let no hate,
no matter how deep or wide, take him in his
solitude. I will not beg his body. I will not weep
and moan. If your will, dear God,
is he be crucified for living, let him die
now in his mother's arms. Let him die now.

TWO

If I say, "I will not mention Him or speak any more in His name," His message becomes a fire burning in my heart, shut up in my bones, and I become weary of holding it in, and I cannot prevail.

Jeremiah 20:9

THE FIRE SHUT UP IN MY BONES

Somewhere in Western Africa, a woman is crossing the street. Or maybe she is in her house nursing a baby. She is Yoruba. We are related. She knows this too because like me she has read history, and even if we had not read history we would still know this familial bond, for this is a plain fact of the world passed down in the body's memory: five hundred years ago men came and severed my life from hers. This fact changes everything. This fact changes nothing. She is still a woman crossing the street or nursing the baby. I am still her kin writing of her. If I returned across the wide ocean, would I find my face in the faces of strangers? Would they invite me in for Joliffe rice and dodo? If the strangers who are my cousins crossed that same ocean, would they make their way to my door? Would I say, "Welcome, beloved. It has been too long"? Would we talk of love and danger? Would we pull out family pictures, scatter the scraps of our lives across the kitchen table? Here is my daughter. Here are my sons. These are our generations. Tell me the stories of all who lie between that moment and your return to me.

This man, my grandfather, owned his own store, was a teacher, and taught his girls to speak their minds. This woman fought for her people and won. This is the daughter of a woman, an ancestor, dead but not forgotten. A French woman, standing on the beach in Barbados, was gathered with a group of enslaved people. Her name was Sadie. She was probably poor and proud. Probably did not speak English. The men who took her did not care about her story, her past, her future. She hated these men and chose an enslaved man for husband. This is the story that has been passed down.

"Once," Great-great-great grandmother Sadie said, "the children were hungry. We were all hungry. So, I took two small pigs from master's sty.

40

Killed and dressed them. One I fed to his family and other I fed to mine. He never knew it."

"But," her grandchildren asked, "Wasn't that stealing? Haven't you said we must never steal?" Sadie would laugh and say, "Stealing? That's not stealing. That's we labor."

Sadie recognized what her grandchildren did not—that her free labor was valuable, that she was valuable, and that even though she was an enslaved woman, her worth did not depend on the estimation of those with legal power over her. Her agency also extended to the community. She shared her payment for her labor, for we labor. That expression came to be used in our family to acknowledge boldness and self-appreciation.

Do you see how we survived? By wit and turpentine? And that story is just the tip of it. Did you wonder about us, dear sister? Did you think of us, dear brother? Or did you get so used to walking about without your arm or leg that you stopped noticing it was gone?

I have noticed your absence and have had to fill it with invention and imagination. I have had to will myself whole. Not severed. Not fragmented. But whole. And to do this, I have leaned into the fire raging in my bones. Truth is a fire I cannot contain. It has to burst out, to be born, to find its own creative joy. This is how I have survived in this land that wants to chew me down, sinews and all, then spit out my bones. This is how I have learned to speak the fire of we labor.

PARABLE

There was once a farmer in Lownesboro, Alabama,
a fertile little shit hill in what they call the black belt.
Let's say he was "white," though that means as much
as saying he was "ostrich." He did okay selling organic
rutabagas and baby lettuces to bistros and vegans. Good
neighbors, beautiful children, a spouse he loved. His life
was as perfect as a real estate commercial. One Tuesday,
strangers kicked in his door, the one his grandfather hewed
with an ax and spit. He grabbed his weapon. But there were so many
even he didn't have enough bullets. And what did these strangers want?
The farmer's best daughter and favorite son. Whom they stole. As if
they had been lawnmowers or bicycles. He called the neighbors together.
Damn if their kin weren't gone too. So, what did he do? He went on.
Even after he heard what happened to all those children and it was worse
than his worst thought's worst thought of what could happen.
He went on. As if the children never existed. Where else could he go?

Several hundred years later, let's say a Tuesday, for circularity,
the progeny of the farmer's daughter and son were sitting at a table
hewn from the bones of their ancestors and spit, when one
of the sons of the sons of the sons who stole them asked,
"Aren't you thankful your people were brought here to our fine country?"
Beloved, do you think those children should have smiled politely,
because they had come so far and all that ugliness was such a long time ago,
about an hour or so, and at least two of them were sitting at the table
(hewn from their bones and they had to scratch like crazy people to get to)
and why be inhospitable or make people uncomfortable over something

some long-dead relative did at least five minutes ago, or why
show ingratitude to a country that gave them the chance to hew tables
out of their bones, then forbade them to sit at them? Or
do you think those children should set that son of a son of a son on fire?

RUNNING IN AMERICA

My son is a runner. Each night
he parts the darkness, his stride
opening and closing like a heart
valve. Opening and closing,
a fist inside my head. I know
the histories that wait for him
like an open grave. In Georgia
men waited for a jogger like my son.
Hunted him with their truck,
then killed him in the street.
Their grandfathers would have taken
him into a field of townspeople,
their boots polished and knives
sharp as teeth, or strung him
upside down like Mary Turner,
belly split, baby crushed beneath
the heels of these good citizens.
Can I scream now? Raze this fetid land
with fire? Count the things
he can't outrun? My son runs on.
He thinks about the girl he saw
yesterday, a test he must take,
the future he is running toward.

MOTHERHOOD

Let's not use a little word like love.
Let's call it Leviathan. That mouth
could swallow generations. Harbor them
in its gut. Better still, let's call it
hurricane, the giant eye peaceful
and omnipotent as God,
the tumult around the eye thick
as peanut butter with destruction
or worry. So unsteady as it clears
a swath through the woods. The world
fills back in. Dangerous places.
Ruthless trees darken the Earth.
Then, let's call it fire
the kind that burns the forest down
emolliates the priest or takes a bullet.
What drops from the body
goes on gazing upwards
as if violence and white vans
were imagination. Where does it end?
This mandoline that shaves everything
on its razor teeth.

'WE WAS GIRLS TOGETHER'*

FOR KDW ON THE DEATH OF HER SON

Hand in hand. Good girls. "Yes,
ma'am," girls. Girls with pink rollers
and dresses long enough. Shoulders
covered in church. Ankles crossed.
Girls with edges. Known to throw
elbows. To flip boys into place
with our new hips. Bare our teeth
in grin or grimace. Girls dancing
in the school gym. Tossing our hair.
our bodies as elegant as satin
gloves. Our hearts certain and unbroken.

*From Toni Morrison's *Sula*

WHEN PRINCE COMES BACK FROM HEAVEN

He will sing to me *Raspberry Beret.*
I will be wearing one. Just like I did
when I sat in the fourth row in love
with him and the boy who held my hand.

I gave that boy his hand back,
But Prince is still my man. Welcome back,
charming one. And yes,
I will ride with you anywhere.

And yes, wear the Afro and purple
suit. Leave the platforms
with your insatiable mother.
Your father will feed the doves.

THE CENSUS MAN WANTS TO KNOW

our race, so the count is right,
so everybody knows how many of us and them
and other might be roaming about and how
do I answer that without adding to a faulty narrative?
Maybe I should say, "Race is the government's category. You pick."
Or maybe I should ask for an etymology given the expansion
of whiteness to folks who have never been white before. It's like
Manifest Destiny redux except with words and not land. Genocide
still hanging in though like a thesis statement or a coda.
Do you think all the Northern Saharan and Middle Eastern folks
know that they have been Europeanized? Is Matt Damon going to play
Osama Bin Laden now? Maybe I should abandon the computer and mail
an explanation, pull-down menus being so inadequate.
I could chronicle a history of rape and coercion. List the Irish great-
grandfather by name. Wax scientific with *homo sapiens* or erudite and hip
with *human*. But even that deserves a footnote since I have to look
among ledgers of livestock and property to fill my family tree.
I'll just mark black. It absorbs all things. Like planets. And light.

COUNTING RACE

"Wait a minute, wait a minute, hold on, just wait a minute," he said, trying to put on an all-knowing smile. "This is called statistical noise."

— CRAIG COBB, white supremacist, disputing a DNA test result that he was 86% European and 14%Sub-Saharan African. Reported by Eric Boodman, statnews.com. 8/16/2017

Day after she walked downtown with her dark husband,
her alabaster arm looped casually through his,
her hazel eyes sparkling with laughter,
my mother ran through those same Selma streets,
down quiet sidewalks, across every friendly
backyard until she reached home
and the welcome of neighbors.
The car of white men pursuing her
wanted a word or two
about her white legs, her blonde head
thrown back, her fingers in his woolly hair. Too bad
they couldn't see her blood.
How can we measure one drop?
By thimble or spoon, by paper bag
or fine-toothed comb? Once, the lexicon noted
the count—hexadecaroon, one-sixteenth black;
octoroon, one whole black grandparent; mulatto, half
and half. We don't like to talk of it that way,

or remember on the 4th of July that Sally Hemings,
quadroon, one-fourth black, bore Thomas Jefferson six children
or think of Strom Thurmond, rabid segregationist, taking
the fifteen-year-old daughter of his maid to bed.
How he hated miscegenation. Even his own blood
in a mulatto daughter's heart could not sway
his rant against her voting rights. How he loved
untainted blood, as much as that man
on the talk show yesterday who wants to build
a white town for whites like him. He smiles
beneath his certainty, his eyes calm
as the dead sea. He does not know purity
is a trap as fake as gerrymandered
districts and black-on-black crime. He does not know,
until the host tells him, the parsing of his blood:
one-seventh black, blacker than an octoroon,
almost as black as my mother, child of a tobacco-colored man,
mixed-race, and a quadroon. I can't remember
what they call that or if I ever knew.

EVEN THE MOON MUST HAVE TROUBLES

Must sometimes climb off its golden swing
drown its sorrows in moon pies
or toss back bottle after bottle
of moonshine with the boys.
At some point it stalks a quiet street
moons the ladies and local preacher,
throws its beams indiscriminately
through every window in town,
howling, as it has seen wolves do,
at the old man who lives inside it
and feasts on green cheese. It marvels
at its round reflection on the lake,
joins a group of revelers, sings loudly
around a campfire, *I see the moon,*
the moon sees me. The moon sees the one
I want to see. "Lunatic," the locals call
as if they have never been moonstruck,
never mooned over the Goddess Ala
or Diana, never waited for the tide
to come in, or go out, or turn
never, not once, lost themselves
to loneliness and lunacy in a lover's arms
beneath its harvest light.

MY SON SAYS THE MOON LANDING WAS A LIE

When I was five, I stole hard candy
from the Winn-Dixie, reached in
an open bin on my way out the door,
dropped the root-beer-flavored prize
in my coat pocket, as if I'd been a thief
my whole life. My mother, holding
my right hand, had no idea of my other's
chicanery or what deception my sweet face
could already manage. At home,
moonlight fell through my window
like a blessing. I ate the little barrel
lying on my bed, still in my yellow coat.

In Sunday school, we learned
the wages of sin are death. Yet no one
ever said how delicious
each dying moment might be.

My son is facing the wall,
poised on one leg. He has lied again.
This is his punishment. His straight back
fortifies the lie he will not give up
for reason or money. Years will pass.
His leg will become a pillar of salt,
his eyes will turn to stone,

and I will break like cooked sugar,
lacking the courage of his small body
or time to stand all day.
I hear myself say, "Truth is all
I ask." The words hang like the moon
above us both, and I remember
I have never liked hard candy
or root beer.

THE TOUR GUIDE WONDERS IF WE ARE PROUD OUR ANCESTORS GOT TO BUILD THIS PLANTATION, DEMOPOLIS, ALABAMA, 2019

FOR HFJ

When she asked,
her eyes pale with hard-
scrabble life, her history
of ingenious men stuck
on replay, this big house
her heritage (had not poverty
been insidious and color-blind)

I saw her,
a child again,
passing the ruthless columns
on her way to school,
a cotton sack dress
hungry for verandas,
even as words hung silent
on our lips, our heads beating
back and forth with no.

54

DETAILS

The first time I saw a man
naked, I was wearing pink
pajamas. The flammable kind
before those were forbidden
to children. A little satin bow,
pre-tied and dotted with a rosebud,
punctuated my collar stretched wide
from washings and ringed by stiff
synthetic lace. My mother had bought them
a week before she died, and I wore them
despite the prickly nylon that bunched
strangely and snagged odd bits
of tiny things. My hair stood
in uncombed tufts. My fingernails dirty
from shooting marbles on the red clay road
with the boys. *Nobody gonna marry*
a Tomboy, girl. I kept playing, crouching low
at the angle of launch, to watch
the beautiful man-made rock bounce
among the pebbles as intensely
as I had watched the window
high above me in the den.
It was long and wide, a slice of light
breaking through in whirly ques
of dust. The sofa was brown plaid. The walls
dark-paneled fake wood.
The space heater still smelled

of melting plastic where, innocent of fire's
ways, I had tended a small meal for my dolls.
My father put ointment on my hand
without a heart to scold, the same hand
a doctor would years later ask if I had ever broken.
Honestly, I could not say,
neither knowing the complete history
of violence against my body nor how
in a brown den lit by a window too high
for my father to fathom where
he stood outside laughing
with a neighbor, a friend of his
happened to lower his trousers and rub
himself against me and my pink pajamas,
long abandoned to some place
I will never precisely recall.

POSSIBLE RESPONSES TO THE NINETEEN-YEAR-OLD
BUTCHER AT THE CORNER STORE IN MY NEIGHBORHOOD
WHO SAID 'YOU LOOK LIKE A GIRL WHO KNOWS WHAT
TO DO WITH SOME COLLARD GREENS'

Country boys can be so charming.
Is that a toothpick in your mouth or a cliché?
I'm going to tell your mother.
What?
Indeed I do sir. Indeed, I do.
May I please look over these pork chops in peace, man?
Two words: Me. Too.
This is why I don't like to shop here.
Didn't you used to date my daughter?
If you don't sit your narrow behind down somewhere—
Do you have any smoked turkey butts back there?
Boy, you ain't ready for my collard greens. Not nearly.

THE LANGUAGE OF JOY

Black woman joy is like this:
Mama said one day long before I was born
she was walking down the street,
foxes around her neck, their little heads
smiling up at her and out at the world
and she was wearing this suit she had saved up
a month's paycheck for after it called to her so seductively
from the window of this boutique. And that suit
was wearing her, keeping all its promises
in all the right places. Indigo. Matching gloves.
Suede shoes dippity-do-dahed in blue.
With tassels! Honey gold. And, Lord, a hat
with plume de peacock, a conductor's baton that bounced
to hip rhythm. She looked so fine she thought
Louis Armstrong might pop up out of those movies
she saw as a child, wipe his forehead and sing
ba da doe doe oh do de doe de doe doe.
And he did. Mama did not sing but she was skiddley-doing that day,
and the foxes grinned, and she grinned
and she was the star of her own Hollywood musical
here with Satchmo who had called Ella over and now they were all
singing and dancing like a free people up Dexter Avenue,
and don't think they didn't know they were walking in the footsteps
of slaves and over auction sites and past where old Wallace
had held onto segregation like a life raft, but this

was not that day. This day was for foxes and hip rhythm,
and musical perfection and folks on the street joining in the celebration
of breath and holiness. And they did too. In color-coordinated ensembles,
they kicked and turned and grinned and shouted like church
or football game, whatever their religious preference. The air
vibrated with music, arms, legs and years of unrequited
sunshine. Somebody did a flip up Dexter Avenue.
It must have been a Nicholas Brother in a featured performance,
and Mama was Miss-Lena-Horne-Dorothy-Dandridge
high stepping up the real estate, ready for her close up.
That's when Mama felt this little tickle. She thought
it might be pent up joy, until a mouse squirmed out
from underneath that fine collar, over that fabulous fur,
jumped off her shoulder and ran down the street.
Left my mama standing there on Dexter Avenue in her blue
suit and dead foxes. And what did Mama do?
Everybody looking at her, robbed by embarrassment?
She said, "It be like that sometimes," then she and Satchmo,
Ella and the whole crew jammed their way home.

MY DAUGHTER SAYS I NEED XANAX: A PARABLE

A dog is chained in a yard. A ring
on her collar stakes her to a length of metal

welded to a thick rod driven deep
into the earth. The long chain makes her world wide

until it's not, until reality snaps and says
it's narrow. The dog is surrounded

by a chain link fence. Through it passersby
taunt her, sure of her limits. And though she is strong

from years of vigorous resistance and her teeth
have been sharpened to razors, and her voice

has grown husky and full, they think she is just a dog
full of bark and tether. But you must remember, Beloved,

chains are meant for snapping, and the day always comes
when even metal rusts and wearies. What will this dog be

in the world then? An avenging angel? An obedient
servant? The tongue of a free woman?

SO MUCH DEPENDS UPON

So much depends
upon

a red wheel
barrow

— William Carlos Williams

the poet's eye.
It turns outward greedy
For every clay hut
bit of eyelet, lost
slipper.

It is easily seduced
by green apples, soup
in a yellow
bowl,

the sloped shoulders
of a man carrying
wood, a woman's hair
falling or her silent
pleasure.

It turns inward,
toward the world's soulful
sound. What sound is that
exactly?

Only the heart and hand
can know, can carry what-
ever the eye gives or make
little lines of wheel-
barrows the stuff of
immortality.

HOW TO MAKE NECKBONES AND RICE

Get a pot. Not Cuisinart. Something deep
and well-seasoned, passed down through generations,
a sacred artifact of hands. Too scratched and bowed
for all the bits to wash away. Put in the meat
full of fat and bone. The shy meat is the meaning
of life, there to be rooted out, earned
by a tenacious tongue. Add salt and pepper,
chopped onion, whatever you got,
and *seasoning.* Water to make the sauce.
Water to stretch the broth. Forget all you have learned:
recipe, sauté, braise. These do not belong here.
Just touch, smell, remembered places. Put your foot
in that pot. Then cook until the bones give up the ghost,
until holiness floats through the house and out
the door. Everybody will know your business,
and envy. Most people throw the rice
into the boiling liquid.
Cook it on the side if you want to put on airs.
Your nose and eyes will tell when it's ready
for the plate. This is all you need for glory:
grain and bone, hot water cornbread,
the flavor of making-do, the altar of your table.

THE MONA LISA IN REAL LIFE

How can we know what will survive before it survives,
or picking up our own likeness by a street artist,
know if we hold a paint-by-numbers fabrication,
a redundancy of someone else's imagination,
or the Mona Lisa, which is much smaller than I imagined,
lonely on its own wall, surrounded by guards and gawkers?
What do they see? Her dark clothes? The spackled face?
That smile unsuited to the pageant circuit. And yet
we love her as much as the Madonna or Madonna.
Why her ? Her and her knowing smirk or indigestion or
imbecility. Who knows? Who knows why we hold so dear
what someone called art, long after the caller has moldered
to nothing. Long after we have abandoned our rote prayers,
and God Himself has grown bored with our ridiculous naming.

ON FIRST LOOKING INTO LUCILLE CLIFTON'S
WORK AFTER AN EDUCATION OF A CERTAIN TYPE

Let's say you find a sketchbook, like Leonardo Da Vinci's,
if he had had a sketchbook, which he did, famously.
After all, what was he supposed to do? Walk around
with good times in his head? That's thoughts, not art,
so even if you didn't know about the sketchbook, you
know about the sketchbook, like the one you've found. This
one is full of gestures—a hand holding a hand,
a turning line that will become a hip or edge
of a sail. Pages of this to that. Someone's scrawled
Lenny from Vinci. Or just *L.* Would you know what
you held in your hands even if you didn't know
what you held in your hands? Or raised on Mona
Lisa, dressed and ready for the Louvre, would you overlook
its beams of light and toss the whole thing out?

FYI TO THE MEN WHO REJECTED A WIKIPEDIA ENTRY ON ME BECAUSE THEY DIDN'T THINK I WAS IMPORTANT ENOUGH

I have taught ten bazillion students to read poetry, birthed
three human beings on lunch breaks, survived erasure before breakfast,
kept my children alive among beasts, enchanted neighbors and enemies,
cooked pound cakes and collards perfectly, fashioned poems into life
preservers, remained in love four hundred years, balanced faith and
rage on my prodigious nose. So, it is predictable you
rejected me with words like *unremarkable* and *too few references
on the Internet*, your semiotics failing always to name me.

Sirs—never heard of these men and no peer among
them—I am too busy to satisfy your yardstick, and
since you lack sufficient laudatory descriptors for me, try these:
stupendous educator, super hero wife and mother, ride or die
friend, bearer of history, lover of sweet potato pie, vengeful
as hell, practitioner of cuss words, American poet, woman, black.

A WOMAN COHABITATES WITH THREE MEN

Not glamorous like it sounds. Two duplicates and the original.
They roar and snort. Beat their chests. Scratch. Always, loud
half-naked. Drop their garments like bread crumbs. Lose things.
Scratch some more. Lose everything beneath and behind. Inexplicable
    spaces
lodge their plunder: tablets, homework, tax returns, a chicken bone
altar. That yellow shoe I will have to find later,
my uterus translated into divining rod. Bodies as battering rams
of sound. Mismatched chromosomes. Weapons of chaos. Truncheons.
    Trebuchets. Terrors.
And yet, I love them. My sweet boys. Feckless warriors—
Destroyers of kitchens. Enemies of my solitude. You have been
too long from conquering. The wilderness calls your names, and
I say go. Take up your armor, gloves and boots.
Sharpen your swing blade, hatchet, and rake. Cover your loins.
Go forth, my darlings, into the feral backyard and slay.

THE FIRST SHALL BE LAST

Once, Mississippi was one of the richest places on Earth,

built on cotton and backs, black bridges
over all waters, the fields of white gold
traversed with railroads and gentility

laid waste by Sherman who lit it all up
like the finger of God dragging a path
of purification across the South's fat

belly, and though that Baptism by fire
did not take, the rivers too occupied by
black bodies plucked from trees or shot

in driveways to truck with salvation,
and though I would not dare, like Milton,
explain God's inscrutable point, I do know

Mississippi is now one of the poorest places on Earth.

ALABAMA THE BEAUTIFUL, AMERICA

Angela Davis was born in Alabama.
So were John Lewis and George Wallace.
So were Zora Neale Hurston and Guicci Mane,
and W. C. Handy and Nat King Cole and Hank Williams.
So many blues and love songs to sing
in this land where Bull Connor
and those dogs were born
and those four little girls in that church
and the men who bombed them
and the Confederacy
and the Civil Rights Movement
and the Black Panthers' blueprint
and the Scottsboro Boys who were accused
and those who bore false witness against them
and Michael Donald who was lynched in 1981
and the boys who lynched him
and the memorial to remember those
lynched all over this habitation of amber
grains waving and waving something
like freedom in straight lines
of assent and then descent
through the wonderland of Alabama,
into the eye of the beholder.

POEM FOR MY NEIGHBOR WHOSE
GOOD INTENTIONS ARE WOLF PELT

This carpet-bagging, gentrifying Aryan mother's son cut
through our neighborhood buying houses. Called himself
a community developer, clipped all the live edges and liberty
neat and bound for himself and his posterity. Declaration
of Independence just doing what it do. And he was pursing
that happiness all right as if it were being stolen or
massa-they-is-running-away down the street with him after
in full stride. Boy, could he smile, unhinge that jaw,
clip it to his ears, wide and sparkly and toothy as an old toothpaste
commercial to buy and sell all abandoned buildings and occupied ones
too. Some folks who knew better could not fly fast enough to miss the
buzz saw of his charm or his sign-on-dotted-line readiness that left them
standing outside their generational house admiring a stranger's yard,
boxes of their shit still stacked on the sidewalk. And then, he painted
his house Alt-White and even black neighbors followed suit, mouthing
something about pure lines and look, as if good intentions could emerge
from a paint can. We all know there is fur beneath the closest of shaves.
Wolf comes uninvited as five o'clock shadow, and even lambs sacrificing
both wool and meat for somebody's pretty cudgel have eyes to see
the coming nick and slaughter. At least, I know very well I do. Fucker.

HOW TO SURVIVE THE APOCALYPSE

Eat grapes daily. Peel them first. Stitch
the skins into bulletproof vests.

Kiss old men. With eyes open. Breathe deeply
Bay Rum and formaldehyde.

Visit grocery stores. Like touring museums. Count
the dwindling rows of kitsch.

Read comic books. And the Apocrypha. Absorb the Torah,
Koran, and Kama Sutra.

Bathe in public. In famous fountains. Drink of lakes, rivers,
the waters of Flint.

Stop making love. Or forgo virginity. Please yourself
incessantly and loudly.

Study penal systems. Japanese internment camps. Post
about the Holocaust, Jim Crow and the Trail of Tears.

Learn to barbeque. To sauté narcissism. Kill politicians
and derelicts for protein.

Survive the lynchings. Like your ancestors. Live
by rage and joy and turpentine.

ACKNOWLEDGMENTS

I would not have finished this book without the kindness of strangers and the help of many friends and family. Thank you to my family: Joseph D. Trimble, who still makes me laugh and makes me happy after thirty-six years—I could not have married anyone but you; my children, Jasmine, Joseph David II, and Joshua—you are the best children in the world. I do not deserve such amazing children. I love you like crazy. To Honorée Fanonne Jeffers, way back friend, ride or die, day one, wise woman, literary goddess, thank you for still being there for me with our marathon conversations even though you are world famous now and everybody knows what a brilliant writer you are. Thank you to my poetry family: Ashley Jones, a young woman with an old soul, for your generosity, your poetic brilliance, and for your unwavering belief in me and my work; Kwoya Fagin Maples and Alina Stefanescue, I want to be like y'all when I grow up—cool, confident, still waters, and dropping that poetic wisdom so beautifully; Randall Horton, my homeboy—I am trying to follow in your footsteps and get my writing groove together—for always encouraging a sistah; Jeanie Thompson, my friend, for schooling me in the business of literature and sharing your amazing knowledge of poets and poetry with me; Susie Paul, for your amazing laugh and for sitting outside that bathroom when we were in Confederate country to make sure no harm came to me; Jennifer Horne and Don Noble, for reading my work and for always supporting me with your advocacy. To Skip and Barbara Jones, thank you for being great hosts, and thanks to the Fairhope Writing Center for the residency that helped me finish this book. Thank you to Arlo Haskell, Freya Hendrickson, Katrin Schumann and the Key

West Literary Seminar for a fabulous space in which to write and for amazing support. Thank you to all the outstanding teachers in whose workshops many of these poems were written or revised—Kevin Young, Rowen Ricardo Phillips, Carl Phillips, Ed Roberson, Dawn Lundy Martin, Cornelius Eady, Dante Micheaux, John Murillo, Patricia Smith, Roger Robinson, Raymond Antrobus, and Malika Booker. Thank you to Nick Makoha, fearless leader/cheerleader/poet and Obsidian Foundation UK for a selecting me as a fellow and the opportunity to work in the company of a family I never knew I had, and thanks to fabulous group D—Jay, Safiya, Adjoa, Sea, Fahad, Nile, Reece, Funmi, and Adam—y'all are the best. Thank you to the National Endowment for the Arts for financial support without which I could not have finished this book. Thank you to Alabama State University for so generously allowing me the time to attend to my writing. To my salon group—Jim, Janet, Foster, Caroline, Tom, Camilla, Catherine, Yvette, Joey, Eileen, David and Mark—y'all make me want to be a better writer just by being you. To Alex, my dear friend and connector of persons extraordinaire, thank you for helping me find a new genre. And finally, thank you to my Sunday School class—Edmund, Juraldine, Miss Kitty, Little Doris, Quintello, Nita, Courtney, Caroline, Jacqueline, and Rev. Dr. Kathy and Rev. Maria—who keep me laughing, grounded and prayed up. May God bless each and every one of you. I wish you peace, joy, and survival.

INDEX OF POEM TITLES

ABOUT THE AUTHOR

JACQUELINE ALLEN TRIMBLE lives and writes in Montgomery, Alabama, where she is a professor of English and chairperson of Languages and Literatures at Alabama State University. Her work has appeared in various online and print publications including *Poetry, Poet Lore, The Rumpus, The Griot, The Offing*, and *The Louisville Review*. She is a Cave Canem fellow, the recipient of a 2017 literary arts fellowship from the Alabama State Council on the Arts, and a 2021 National Endowment for the Arts Creative Writing Fellow (Poetry).